FAMOUS TRACKS

Jeff Burton

Dale Earnhardt Jr.

Famous Finishes

Famous Tracks

Kenny Irwin Jr.

Jimmie Johnson

The Labonte Brothers

Lowriders

Monster Trucks & Tractors

Motorcycles

Off-Road Racing

Rockcrawling

Tony Stewart

The Unsers

Rusty Wallace

FAMOUS TRACKS

Al Pearce

CHELSEA HOUSE
P U B L I S H E R S
A Haights Cross Communications Company ®
Philadelphia

Cover Photo: The field passes by while other race cars head for the pits in this view of a NASCAR event at Martinsville Speedway, Martinsville, Virginia.

CHELSEA HOUSE PUBLISHERS

VP, New Product Development   Sally Cheney
Director of Production   Kim Shinners
Creative Manager   Takeshi Takahashi
Manufacturing Manager   Diann Grasse

STAFF FOR FAMOUS TRACKS

Editorial Assistant Sarah Sharpless
Production Editor Bonnie Cohen
Photo Editor Pat Holl
Series Design and Layout Hierophant Publishing Services/EON PreMedia

http://www.chelseahouse.com

A Haights Cross Communications ◤ Company ®

First Printing

1   3   5   7   9   8   6   4   2

Library of Congress Cataloging-in-Publication Data

Pearce, Al, 1942-
   Famous tracks / Al Pearce.
      p. cm. --(Race car legends. Collector's edition)
   Includes bibliographical references and index.
   ISBN 0-7910-8692-5
  1.Racetracks (Automobile racing)--United States--Juvenile literature. 2.Automobile racing--United States--Juvenile literature.I. Title. II. Series.
GV1033.P43 2005
796.72'06'8--dc22

                                                    2005012288

All links and Web addresses were checked and verified to be correct at the time of publication. Because of the dynamic nature of the Web, some addresses and links may have changed since publication and may no longer be valid.

TABLE OF CONTENTS

CRANK UP THE BULLDOZERS

It's been said that America's most enthusiastic race fans are people with open land and a bulldozer. Eventually, they'll climb up on that bulldozer and build themselves a speedway.

That's what Henry Clay Earles did near Martinsville, Virginia, in 1947. Harold Brasington did the same thing at Darlington, South Carolina, in 1950. Bill France Sr. had bulldozers and open land, so he built speedways at Daytona Beach, Florida, in 1959, and at Talladega, Alabama, in 1969. Curtis Turner and Bruton Smith built a speedway near Charlotte, North Carolina, in 1960; then, Smith built one near Fort Worth, Texas, in 1997. Since the late 1940s, in fact, thousands of people have spent countless days and nights turning open land into speedways. Many of these speedways fail after only a few years. Others are still around and attract fans to races all over the United States.

Since its debut in 1949, the NASCAR **Nextel Cup** series (formerly known as the **Winston Cup series**) has visited 171 different speedways in 36 states and two Canadian cities. Alaska, Colorado, Hawaii, Idaho, Mississippi, Missouri, Minnesota, Montana, New Mexico, North Dakota, Rhode

Island, Utah, Vermont, and Wyoming are still waiting for their first major race. NASCAR's second-level Busch series raced in Mexico City in March of 2005, and many people think the Cup Series will eventually visit Canada and Mexico as well. (**NASCAR** stands for National Association for Stock Car Auto Racing.)

One thing separates speedways from other major-league sports facilities: no two speedways are alike because speedways aren't designed or built to a set of standard measurements. Every football field (for example) is 100 yards long, with two 10-yard end zones. The distance between bases on every baseball diamond is 90 feet. Every college and professional basketball court is 94 feet long, and the baskets are always 10 feet above the floor. All tennis courts and international soccer fields are the same size. But speedways can be any length and width, depending on what the builder wants.

Some builders want long speedways with steeply banked turns. They think fans enjoy seeing cars going two-wide and three-wide at almost 200 miles per hour. Among the most famous "super tracks" are the 2.5-mile Daytona International Speedway in Florida and the 2.66-mile Talladega Superspeedway in Alabama. These tracks are long enough to accommodate 100,000 fans along the **frontstretch** and upward of 75,000 more in the turns and along the **backstretch**. These speedways attract sellout crowds, large television audiences, and hundreds from the media.

Other builders want speedways somewhat shorter and with lower turns. Among these are the 1.5-mile facilities near Charlotte, Atlanta, Fort Worth, Kansas City, and Las Vegas. The 2-mile banked tracks near Jackson, Michigan, and Fontana, California, see speeds only slightly slower than those at Daytona Beach and Talladega. Fans often enjoy these tracks more because more of the driver's skill is involved and the competition is closer.

NASCAR cars run three-wide on the high-banked turns during practice at the Talladega Superspeedway in Talladega, Alabama.

Still other builders want short speedways, between one-half and three-quarters of a mile long. They like the idea of cars being bunched together for an entire race. NASCAR's short tracks are at Martinsville and Richmond in Virginia, and Bristol, Tennessee. Many fans prefer these "bullrings" over the larger and faster speedways. These tracks usually have more crashes because the cars are always close together at fairly slow speeds. One mistake often leads to an accident among six or more cars.

The shortest speedway ever to host a major race was the one-fifth of a mile Islip Speedway, near New York City. The longest were the four-mile road course at Elkhart Lake, Wisconsin, and a four-mile highway/beach course in Daytona Beach, Florida. During NASCAR's first 11 years, most of its major races were on short speedways covered by dirt or

Fans enjoy the Firestone Indy 225, the last race held at Nazareth International Speedway in Nazareth, Pennsylvania. The historic track closed down after the 2004 season.

red clay. Many were at state or county fairgrounds, using the same ovals that hosted horse races. It wasn't until the mid-1960s that paved speedways became more popular. Even so, dirt-track racing was an important part of NASCAR for more than 20 years. Richard Petty won the last dirt-track race at Raleigh, North Carolina, in September 1970. The next year, all 48 NASCAR races were on paved tracks. That was the first sign that stock car racing was growing up.

Many speedways that thrived in the sport's early years closed. Owners found that their property was worth far more to developers than it was as a speedway. Among the speedways that were bought out were those at Langhorne,

A road course offers more challenges to the driver than the typical oval track. This aerial view of Watkins Glen, New York, was taken during the 1967 Grand Prix. The race drew a crowd of 85,000.

Pennsylvania; Riverside, California; Bridgehampton, New York; and Ontario, California. In recent years, Nazareth Speedway in Pennsylvania, North Carolina Speedway at Rockingham, and North Wilkesboro Speedway in North Carolina have closed.

Several American cities have speedways near their downtown, including Daytona Beach, Richmond, Indianapolis, and Dover. But most of today's major speedways are away from business and residential areas. The road courses at Watkins Glen, New York, and Sonoma, California, are miles from the nearest population centers. There's nothing near the speedways at Pocono, Pennsylvania; Loudon, New Hampshire;

DID YOU KNOW?

The Talladega Superspeedway at Dry Valley, Alabama, is among NASCAR's most famous tracks. It stretches for 2.66 miles, the longest oval in all of American motorsports. Its turns are banked at a daunting 33 degrees, even steeper than the banking at Daytona International Speedway (DIS). Its qualifying record of 212.809 miles per hour is more than 2 miles per hour faster than any track in stock car racing. It's been the scene of some of stock car racing's most exciting races and breathtaking finishes. Six drivers have gotten their only career victories at the facility originally called the Alabama International Motor Speedway.

But the track between Birmingham and Anniston, in eastern Alabama, has had its share of troubles and tragedy. In September of 1969, two days before its first-ever race, many of NASCAR's most famous drivers loaded up and went home because they felt the track was unsafe. Two drivers, one motorsports executive, a crewman for Richard Petty, and several fans have died there. Famous driver Davey Allison died and two passengers were injured when his helicopter crashed in the infield. Several fans were injured by debris when Bobby Allison's car almost cleared the frontstretch fence in a scary 1987 accident. A disturbed fan snatched the pace car and went on a joy ride moments before a race in the mid-1980s. Penske Racing executive Don Miller lost his right leg in a pit accident and former championship driver Bobby Isaac quit mid-race because (he said) he heard voices telling him to park the car. Talladega has been the scene of so many scary, multi-car accidents that it coined the term "The Big One" to describe huge wrecks.

According to old-timers, there's a reason for the speedway's bizarre reputation. A long-held legend says leaders of the Creek Indian Nation cursed Dry Valley when they were forced to relocate to Oklahoma in 1838–1839. The land they'd lived on and cultivated for generations included ground sacred to their religion and a burial ground. It's only a legend, but considering the strange things that have happened there, maybe the speedway site is cursed after all.

Talladega, Alabama; and Martinsville, Virginia. The speedway at Homestead, Florida, is 30 miles from Miami. The speedway at Hampton, Georgia, is 30 miles from Atlanta and the one at Jackson, Michigan, is 80 miles from Detroit. The Chicagoland Speedway is 45 miles from Chicago and the Kansas Speedway is 30 miles from Kansas City. It seems a certainty that future speedways will be built well away from built-up areas.

All but two of NASCAR's 36 major races in 2005 were on 20 oval tracks. Teams also raced on two road circuits. The tracks at Sonoma and Watkins Glen are different from the ovals that fans are accustomed to seeing. On ovals, drivers turn left and seldom brake hard except for emergencies and pit stops. On road courses, drivers must turn left and right, shift gears, and use their brakes continually. The tracks often go up and down, making racing more challenging. Watkins Glen has 11 turns and measures 2.45 miles. The Sonoma track has eight turns and is 1.99 miles.

In recent years, NASCAR has expanded in almost every area of the United States. Only the Northwest and the Great Plains, between Kansas City and Denver, don't have major speedways. Officials hope to build one in the Northwest within a few years and another close to New York City within 10 years. The people with the bulldozers are standing by. All they need is the open land.

2

MARTINSVILLE: A PLACE IN NASCAR HISTORY

Martinsville Speedway in Virginia holds a special place in stock car racing history. It's the only active speedway that hosted an event during the first Nextel Cup season of 1949. NASCAR organized eight races for street-legal, family sedans that year. Seven of the eight were on dirt tracks, and five of them were on tracks shorter than a mile. Fifty-six years later, Martinsville is the only speedway among the original eight still going strong.

The other seven closed years ago. One was a rough and rutted three-quarter miler in Charlotte, North Carolina. Another was a 4-mile track near Daytona Beach, Florida, that used part of a paved public highway and part of the wide, hard-packed beach. There were 1-mile facilities at Hillsboro, North Carolina, and at Langhorne, Pennsylvania. The other four were one-half mile speedways at Hamburg, New York; Pittsburgh, Pennsylvania; North Wilkesboro, North Carolina; and Martinsville. The sixth race of that first season was a 200-lap, 100-miler on September 25 at Martinsville.

Martinsville Speedway in Martinsville, Virginia, has 500-lap
Nextel Cup races and 250-lap Craftsman Truck series races.

Today, the popular little speedway in rural Virginia has
500-lap Nextel Cup races and 250-lap Craftsman Truck
series races each April and October. On separate weekends
in the fall, it also has races for NASCAR's fast and exciting
Modified Tour cars and the popular Late Model Stock Cars.
It has also hosted races for NASCAR's Busch, All-Pro, and
Daytona Dash series. It tried to run sports car, open-wheel
championship car, Midget, and motorcycle races in the 1950s.
The fans wanted nothing but NASCAR stock cars.

Martinsville has been described as "a large paperclip."
Its parallel straightaways are flat and less than a quarter-mile
long. Its short, tight turns are banked a modest 12 degrees. It's
the shortest and slowest of the 22 speedways with Cup races.
Its qualifying record of 97.513 miles per hour is almost

Martinsville is the shortest and slowest of the speedways with Cup races. The paper clip-shaped track has parallel straightaways that are less than a quarter-mile long.

31 mph slower than at Bristol Motor Speedway, the tour's second-slowest track. Even so, Martinsville is a difficult test for drivers and crews because the 43 cars are always close to each other. It's like high-speed, rush-hour traffic on a narrow city street. That close competition is why Martinsville is among fans' most popular tracks.

"You know you're going to have your hands full at Martinsville," said Darrell Waltrip, an 11-time winner there.

You have to be patient and use your head. You can't get mad when you run into somebody or when some-body runs into you. If you do, you'll be mad at some-body all day long. You're always in heavy traffic. There's always somebody in front of you and behind you. There's always somebody beside you. You can't relax even a second because faster cars will lap you. Whether you win or lose, you've done a day's work at Martinsville.[1]

Virginia native Henry Clay Earles built the track shortly after completing a two-year Navy hitch after World War II. Like many Southerners in the mid-1940s, he thought this new-fangled curiosity called "stock car racing" was exciting. He and long-time friend Sam Rice attended several dirt-track races in Virginia and North Carolina in 1946 and 1947. They were impressed by the racing and surprised at how many people attended. They came to believe that racing might be a good way to make a living. (Years later, Earles said he'd probably overestimated the attendance at those races. By then, of course, it was too late to change his career path.)

Earles, Rice, and mutual friend Henry Lawrence spent several weeks in 1947 looking for a place to build a speedway. They found it south of Martinsville, near the Virginia-North Carolina state line. It was about 30 acres in a small valley, barely enough for a half-mile track and some grandstands. Owned by the McCrickard family, the land was lined on two sides by small trees and underbrush. Railroad tracks were along another side. The fourth side was bordered by a steep hill. They used Rice's earth-moving equipment to shape their track in the spring and summer. Each man planned to spend $10,000 (a sizeable investment in 1947) but ended up spending twice that much. They didn't have enough time or money to put up fences, so many fans simply walked through the woods and watched the first race without paying.

Earles and former racer Bill France Sr. organized a 100-lap race for Modified Stock Cars on September 7, 1947. Martinsville had only 750 seats, but several thousand fans stood in the infield and throughout the property. They saw World War II veteran Red Byron beat Bob Flock, Ed Samples, Jack Etheridge, and Fred Mahon in the 50-miler. Three months later, in Daytona Beach, Florida, France Sr. created NASCAR to control and promote stock car racing. NASCAR staged 58 Modified Stock Car races in 1948, including one at Martinsville on July 4. Almost 4,000 fans watched Fonty Flock beat Pee Wee Martin, Buck Baker, Bill Blair, and Tim Flock in a 100-lap, 50-mile race.

In 1949, France Sr. realized that fans preferred street-legal, family sedans to Modified Stock Cars. He quickly created an eight-race schedule for what he called **Strictly Stock**. On Sunday afternoon, September 25, 1949, almost 10,000 fans were at Martinsville Speedway for the sixth race of that eight-race season. Byron beat Lee Petty and Ray Erickson by three laps. Clyde Minter was 10 laps behind and Bill Blair was 14 behind. Earles and France Sr. copromoted a pair of 200-lap races each in 1950, 1951, 1952, 1953, and 1954. The track was popular with fans, but Earles couldn't keep dust and dirt from settling on them. Early in 1955, shortly after Tim Flock beat Lee Petty, Junior Johnson, Jimmie Lewallen, and Bob Welborn in a 200-lapper, Earles decided to pave the track. Several friends and associates considered it unwise since dirt-track racing was popular. France Sr. thought paving would ruin the track, but Earles convinced him that paving would make it even more popular.

The work was done in the summer and early fall of 1955. At the time, Martinsville became one of only three paved NASCAR tracks and the only one shorter than a mile. (The others were a one-mile oval at Raleigh, North Carolina, and the famous 1.375-mile oval at Darlington, South Carolina.) Billy Myers won Martinsville's first paved race, a 100-lapper for Sportsman cars in early October. Two weeks later, on

 It happens at least once or twice each day during every race weekend at Martinsville Speedway. A long, slow-moving freight train rumbles within 50 feet of the backstretch grandstand. Trains have become as familiar to NASCAR fans at Martinsville as the flowers, shrubs, and bushes around the half-mile speedway in southern Virginia.

The railroad tracks were there when the late H. Clay Earles built his speedway in 1947. They had been in place since the late 1800s when passenger trains were the easiest way to get around Virginia. The tracks left Roanoke, Virginia, worked their way through Martinsville, past the speedway, and on to Winston-Salem, North Carolina, for connections to other southern cities. Passenger service was discontinued in the 1950s, but Norfolk Southern freight trains continue carrying coal, new cars, and agricultural products along the line.

In time, the speedway and the railroad began outgrowing each other. One concern was the thousands of fans staying overnight in RVs or camping out behind the

(Continued)

October 16, Speedy Thompson beat Welborn, Jim Paschal, Herb Thomas, and Jim Reed in a **Grand National** race. More than 12,000 fans, a speedway record at that time, braved threatening weather to see the "new" speedway.

Earles created another huge story the following year. He extended his two Nextel Cup races from 200 laps to 500 backstretch. They had to cross the tracks to reach the speedway, often when trains were approaching. In addition, the speedway needed the land behind the backstretch for another high-rise grandstand. But the railroad tracks were almost exactly where builders needed to put the foundation for the grandstands. In the late 1990s, speedway and railroad officials began studying plans to relocate the tracks.

"The easiest part of the whole thing was actually moving the tracks," said speedway president Clay Campbell, grandson of H. Clay Earles. "The paperwork and insurance concerns took longer than grading and physically relocating the tracks. We had to be sure the 't's were crossed and the 'i's were dotted. Everybody thought we should do it, but it wasn't an easy project."

It happened in 2005. Railroad workers spent months preparing a new roadbed almost 250 feet from the old one. The new line cuts the campground almost in half, meaning only half as many fans have to cross the tracks. Because of the relocation, the new grading and the slope of the land, some fans in the grandstands may not even see the trains passing. Sadly, another long-time tradition has fallen victim to progress.

laps, from 100 miles to 250 miles. At the time, no half-mile track was hosting races longer than 200 miles. Earles felt the number "500" was special enough to attract thousands of new fans. He was proved right when 20,000 fans jammed into his speedway on May 20, 1956, to see Buck Baker beat Thompson, Lee Petty, Paul Goldsmith, and Gwyn Staley. Since then, every major race at the speedway has been for 500 laps.

Martinsville Speedway's high-rise grandstands surround the concrete racing surface, offering close-up views of the exciting action.

Despite its modest size, Martinsville is among America's best-run speedways. It has 91,000 permanent seats, mostly in high-rise grandstands surrounding the concrete racing surface. Dozens of VIP suites overlook the frontstretch and Turns 1 and 2. High-rise grandstands in Turn 2 and Turns 3–4 offer panoramic views of the close and exciting competition. Every Cup race is sold out with a waiting list for tickets. The speedway offers the same hospitality today that Earles displayed in 1947, when he apologized to fans for the dust and clay kicked up in his first race. He made his track one of America's prettiest by planting flowers, shrubs, and bushes throughout the property. He stocked a small, pretty lake near the main entrance with fish, ducks, and turtles. Many fans consider the spring race, with flowers and bushes in full bloom, among NASCAR's most pleasant weekends.

"My grandfather visited other tracks and thought some of them were an eyesore," said speedway president William Clay Campbell, grandson of Clay Earles.

> From the very beginning, he thought fans should feel at home here. That meant clean rest rooms and nice homey touches around the track. If you look at very old pictures, you'll see rose bushes growing over the outhouses in the infield. Grandaddy was very meticulous, from the way he dressed to the way he kept his cars and to his race track. It was a point of pride that people left here talking not only about a good race, but how neat and clean everything was.

Earles retired in 1988 and named Campbell his successor. Earles stayed active in track management right up until his death in November of 1999 at age 86. Five years later, Campbell sold his speedway to International Speedway Corporation (ISC), one of NASCAR's closest "cousins." ISC kept Campbell as president and urged him to continue improving its newest property. Today, the little, one-half mile speedway remains one of America's most enduring sports facilities, sort of the Wrigley Field or Fenway Park of motorsports. Who would have imagined such a bright future back in 1947?

3

DARLINGTON: TOO TOUGH TO TAME

Major-league stock car racing was barely a year old when Harold Brasington began building a speedway that would change the face of the sport. In 1949, NASCAR organized eight races for its new and growing "Strictly Stock" class. The races covered 100 to 200 laps on short tracks that were covered by dirt or clay. The street-legal, family sedans in this new series seldom reached 100 miles per hour.

Brasington was a former racer from Darlington, a small farming town in northeastern South Carolina. He wanted a speedway that would bring fame to Darlington like the Indianapolis Motor Speedway brought to Indianapolis, Indiana. He'd attended an Indy 500 and was impressed by the massive, four-sided, 2.5-mile facility. (Indy was the world's largest speedway at the time). Brasington was also impressed by the number of fans attending the Indy 500 and how much money they spent. He wanted to attract a similar gathering to his hometown. But, instead of open-wheel "champ cars" so popular in the Midwest, he wanted his 500-mile race to feature stock cars.

Many people thought Brasington was crazy when he broke ground early in 1950. He wanted to be ready by Labor Day, the first Monday in September. He and several friends

Darlington Raceway in Darlington, South Carolina, was designed with broad, sweeping, moderately banked turns. NASCAR Nextel Cup cars are shown racing under the lights.

used his road-grading equipment to shape the track on 70 acres of farmland between Darlington and nearby Hartsville. It was a simple process: Brasington designed Darlington Raceway on paper napkins from a local café. He sketched a 1.25-mile speedway with broad, sweeping, moderately banked turns. Brasington wanted his new facility to be suitable for champ cars and stock cars.

Everything went fine until he faced an unexpected problem. Sherman Ramsey, the farmer who sold Brasington the land, raised minnows in a small pond near the construction site. If Brasington shaped the western end similar to how he'd shaped the eastern end, Ramsey's minnow pond would be destroyed. Impressed by the farmer's plea, Brasington went back and redrew the design for the western end of his speedway. He made that end sharper, higher-banked and shorter, thus preserving the pond. That's why Darlington has its unique and challenging egg shape. Turns 1–2 at the eastern end are broad, sweeping, and moderately banked; turns 3–4 at the western end are narrow, tight, and higher-banked.

Darlington Raceway's unique challenge is its egg shape. The turns at the western end are tighter and higher-banked than the turns at the eastern end. The infield is shown full of tents and trailers during the Southern 500 race in 2003.

"The difference in the turns is why Darlington's always been so difficult," says Ricky Rudd, winner of the track's 1991 spring race. "Most speedways are about the same at each end. If your car handles good at one end, it'll probably handle good at the other. But Darlington's different. You can be good at one end and bad at the other because the ends are so different. The other thing is, you don't have time to relax. Darlington's so different at each end and so narrow, there's no room for error. Sometimes it seems like the walls jump out and grab you. No question about it, Darlington's the toughest place we race. It was built 50-some years ago for cars running 75 to 85 miles per hour. Now, we're running about twice that fast."[2]

The track had 9,000 concrete seats when it opened in September of 1950. The Southern 500 was stock car racing's first paved race and its first 500-mile race. With promotion and organizational help from NASCAR president Bill France Sr., the historic event attracted 80 teams. Brasington limited the starting field to 75, by far the largest stock car field to that point. He started the cars three-wide in 25 rows, an unmistakable tribute to the famous three-wide grid for the Indy 500. France worried about the number of cars and the race distance. He didn't think most street-legal cars could last 500 miles on a hot and humid Monday afternoon. He also worried that fans might become disappointed and stop attending races if the 500 turned out poorly.

Junie Donlavey of Richmond, Virginia, owned a small, low-budget race team in 1950. He was impressed that someone had built a paved, banked, 1.25-mile speedway in a small South Carolina town. He and some of his friends decided to enter the first Southern 500. "Nobody had heard of anything like a 500-mile race for stock cars," Donlavey said years later. "I mean, we couldn't even imagine something like that. Up until then, every big race had been on short dirt tracks. When they scheduled a 500-mile race for Labor Day weekend, we started getting ready. Since nobody else had ever raced there, we figured we had as good a chance as anybody. But the big thing was just to be part of it. You can't imagine what a big deal it was for Southern stock car teams to have a 500-mile race."[3]

Indeed, the first Southern 500 was NASCAR's biggest event to that point. It even created a fair amount of interest across America, which was beginning to take notice of NASCAR. Brasington posted a record payout of $25,000 and scheduled 15 days for practice and qualifying. Curtis Turner ran 82.034 miles per hour to earn the pole, on the inside of the front row. Although he won the pole, he wasn't the fastest qualifier. Wally Campbell took that honor at 82.400 mph. But Campbell started only sixtieth since he qualified several days after time trials began. He even started behind Johnny Mantz, whose speed of 73.460 mph was the slowest among the 75 cars in the race.

Fans began arriving in northeastern South Carolina several days before the race. It wasn't long until every motel and hotel within 50 miles of Darlington was filled. When more than 6,000 fans were stranded without rooms, speedway executives opened the infield. Many fans spent Saturday and Sunday nights camping out or sleeping in their cars. More than 25,000 fans watched the race, by far NASCAR's largest crowd to that point. Gober Sosebee, Curtis Turner, and Cotton Owens traded the lead three times in the first 49 laps. Johnny Mantz took over at lap 50 and stayed ahead the rest of the 400-lap, 500-mile race. He finished nine laps ahead of Fireball Roberts and won more than $10,000.

Mantz used a unique strategy. He expected most of his rivals to run hard from the start in hopes of impressing fans and the media. He didn't think that would work for long. Cars of that era weren't capable of running 500 miles at high speed. So Mantz chose a slower, safer, and more conservative pace. Instead of outrunning everyone, he hoped to outlast them, which he did. He also knew tire wear would be important. He chose truck-quality tires that were harder and more durable than "street" tires. In addition, his winning Plymouth was smaller and lighter than the Oldsmobiles, Cadillacs, Mercurys, and Lincolns in the field. He didn't have many tire problems and covered the 500 miles in 6 hours, 38 minutes.

That first Southern 500 proved that properly prepared, street-legal, family sedans could race for 500 miles. A year later, more than 40,000 fans watched 82 cars in the second annual Southern 500. It took only a few years for the annual Labor Day weekend race to become NASCAR's most important event. It was stock

DID YOU KNOW?

Two of the first rules at every speedway are fairly obvious: stay off the wall and don't bang up your race car. For many years, though, one of the first rules at Darlington Raceway was dramatically different: lean gently against the wall and use it to your advantage.

In the mid-1950s, some NASCAR drivers discovered that the fastest line around the egg-shaped track was in the high lane, within 12 to 18 inches from the wall. Later, quite by mistake, they realized they could go even faster by leaning the right-rear fender against the steel guardrail in Turns 3 and 4. That light contact helped them get a better "jump" off Turn 4 by using the steel railing almost like a "slingshot" down the frontstretch. Before long, getting a "Darlington stripe" became the most popular way of getting around the track. You probably weren't going very fast if you didn't have a stripe along the right side of your car.

"We actually built our cars with more bracing in the right-rear because we knew what was going to happen," said team-owner Junie Donlavey, who fielded a car in the first Southern 500 at Darlington in September of 1950. "The really good drivers knew how to lean against the wall with just enough pressure. If they leaned too hard, they'd mess up the car and lose time. If they didn't lean quite hard enough, they wouldn't be fast enough. There was a fine line between running fast and crashing. The ability to get that so-called 'Darlington stripe' is what separated the great drivers from everybody else."

The famous speedway in Darlington, South Carolina was built in 1950 at 1.25 miles. It was re-measured more accurately in 1953 at 1.375 miles. It was measured even more accurately at its current 1.366 miles in time for the 1970 Mountain Dew Southern 500. The track had only one strand of highway-like guardrail until the early 1970s, when a second strand was added. When the concrete walls went up in the late-1980s, it brought an end to the "Darlington stripe" era.

Mark Martin's pit crew changes tires during the Southern 500 at Darlington Raceway. Tire quality has figured into racing strategy since Johnny Mantz won the first Southern 500 in 1950.

car racing's only 500-miler until 1958 when the 1-mile track at Trenton, New Jersey, hosted a 500-miler. Darlington was the only 500-miler in the South until the 1959 Daytona 500. The speedway was changed slightly and measured at 1.375 miles in 1953. It was measured again at its current 1.366-mile length in 1970. Brasington added a spring race in 1960, and the track hosted two races a year through 2004.

Darlington Raceway is among the handful of NASCAR tracks with an easily identifiable nickname. For years, because of its black asphalt, it was called "The Lady in Black." But the nickname that seems more appropriate emerged several years ago. Four words say it all: "Too Tough To Tame."

4

DAYTONA BEACH: THE ROSE BOWL OF RACING

Daytona International Speedway (DIS) in Daytona Beach, Florida, is stock car racing's most famous track. It's as important to racing as the Rose Bowl is to college football. It's almost as well-known as Yankee Stadium, Madison Square Garden, and Wimbledon. Many racers consider their career incomplete unless they've won at least once at "The Beach."

The speedway hosts more than a dozen major events each year, more than any track in America. The annual Speed Week program in February opens the country's racing season. It includes a 24-hour sports car race through the speedway's infield road course and around most of its stock car track. That's followed by eight stock car races, including the Daytona 500. Every March, approximately 150,000 motorcycle enthusiasts gather for motocross and motorcycle races during the speedway's famous Bike Week gathering. NASCAR returns for a sports car race and two more stock car races early in July. The speedway's season closes in December with a series of world championship go-kart races.

Daytona International Speedway in Daytona Beach, Florida, is stock car racing's most famous track. The field of 43 cars take the green flag to start the 47th Daytona 500 and the 2005 NASCAR Nextel Cup series season.

The Daytona Beach area is considered the world's "birthplace of speed." Men began racing primitive cars on its 20 miles of wide, hard-packed beaches in 1902. Racing pioneers Alexander Winton and Ransom Olds preferred Florida's good weather to the salt flats of Utah. In March of 1935, Sir Malcolm Campbell brought his Bluebird from England in hopes of reaching 300 miles per hour. After reaching only 276.82 mph, he announced he was moving all future land-speed runs to Bonneville, Utah. After more than 35 years as a racing destination, Daytona Beach lost its only claim to fame.

City officials quickly replaced the land-speed runs with a stock car race for family sedans. The cars raced southward along a public street near the beach, turned left onto the beach, and raced northward. Drivers completed one lap of the 4-mile course by turning left and returning to the public highway. The city lost money on that race and dropped plans for more races. The local Elks Club lost money when it organized and promoted a race in 1937. Things improved somewhat when driver/businessman Bill France Sr. and restaurant owner Charlie Reese promoted two races in 1938. They successfully promoted ten more stock car races spanning the next three years. Their plans for more races in 1942 were dashed when America entered World War II in December of 1941.

Shortly after the war ended in June of 1945, France Sr. resumed promoting races. He became so successful that thousands of fans visited Daytona Beach each February for the highway/beach races. In time, as homes and businesses emerged along the beach, he saw the need for a permanent track. He wanted one to accommodate tens of thousands of fans like Darlington Raceway in South Carolina, and Indianapolis Motor Speedway in Indiana. In February of 1954, he announced that the 1955 Speed Week program would be the last on the highway/beach course. He revealed plans for a long, paved, high-banked speedway on 500 acres of swampland west of the city. France Sr. got $35,000 seed money from Texas oilman Clint Murchison, future owner of the Dallas Cowboys.

This six-car chain reaction crash happened during Daytona Beach's Golden Anniversary "Speed Week" in 1953. By 1959 the race had moved from the highway/beach course to the paved, high-banked speedway.

Even so, the work took much longer than anyone expected. France Sr. faced opposition from citizens worried that a speedway big enough for tens of thousands of fans would spoil their city. The Civil Aeronautics Board thought the speedway might interfere with activities at the nearby airport. Financial roadblocks and design problems delayed groundbreaking until early 1958. France Sr. grew so impatient that he considered moving his new NASCAR headquarters and his planned speedway to West Palm Beach. He reconsidered when city officials helped clear some obstacles. In the meantime, he kept attracting huge crowds and national attention to the February races on the highway/beach course.

France Sr. and architect Charles Moneypenny designed the new track at 2.5 miles. It was the same length as the Indianapolis Motor Speedway and more than a mile longer than any other NASCAR speedway. They banked the turns 31 degrees, three stories high and almost too steep to walk up. They banked the frontstretch 18 degrees and the backstretch 6 degrees. They made the speedway a **tri-oval** by pulling the frontstretch slightly away from the backstretch. That meant fans along the frontstretch could see cars approaching from Turn 4 and watch them heading into Turn 1. The turns were steeply banked for two reasons: cars run faster on banked tracks and fans see them better because they're more visible when they go up the **banking**.

"I'll never forget the first time I saw the speedway in February of 1959," says retired seven-time NASCAR champion Richard Petty.

> Nobody had seen anything bigger than Darlington, which we always thought was pretty dad-gum big. And Daytona was banked more than anything we'd ever seen. When we came through the tunnel and saw the turns, I thought, "Man, how are we gonna race up there?" I think some of the older drivers were more nervous than I was. I hadn't raced very much [he was 21 at the time], so I didn't have as much to un-learn. Daytona was new to everybody, so I was starting out pretty even. I was a rookie, but Daytona made me as good as everybody else.

Most sports end their seasons with playoffs and a championship game. NASCAR opens its season with the Daytona

Daytona International Speedway underwent a major remodeling effort in 2004. The speedway generates hundreds of millions of dollars for the area's economy every year.

500, its most important race. It caps two full weeks of racing at the speedway. Almost 200,000 fans now attend the 500, more than five times the number of people at the first one in 1959. The speedway has added high-rise grandstand seats and dozens of VIP suites several times. Its grandstands ring the frontstretch between Turns 4 and 1, and a huge grandstand sits along the 3,200-foot backstretch. Thousands of fans camp out or stay in recreational vehicles in the infield. Hotels and motels within 75 miles of Daytona Beach are filled. It's estimated that the speedway generates several hundred million dollars for the area's economy every year.

DIS has been the site of many of NASCAR's most memorable finishes. Officials spent several days reviewing news film and photographs of the finish of the first Daytona 500. Lee Petty and Johnny Beauchamp finished so close together that nobody knew who'd won. (This was before finish-line cameras, electronic scoring, or television broadcasts.) France Sr. and several officials sent Beauchamp to Victory Lane thinking he had won. But they reversed themselves several days later and named Petty the winner. Ironically, Petty never got the winner's trophy.

The 1976 Daytona 500 also ended in a spectacular fashion. Hall of Fame drivers Richard Petty (son of Lee Petty) and David Pearson banged together in Turn 4 on the last lap. They bounced against the outside wall and began spinning a quarter-mile from the finish line. Petty's car stalled, and he couldn't drive it any farther. Despite major damage to its nose, Pearson kept his car running. He took the checkered flag at 20 miles per hour for his only Daytona 500 victory. Petty's crewmen rushed from the pits to push him over the line for second-place finish. Neither driver was angry since they realized that winning the Daytona 500 was worth whatever it took.

Three years later, Cale Yarborough and the Allison brothers created another memorable Daytona 500 finish. Yarborough and Donnie Allison made contact in Turn 2 on the last lap. They kept hitting each other along the backstretch, neither man willing to give up. When they finally crashed for good in Turn 3, Richard Petty passed them en route to winning. As Petty celebrated his seventh career Daytona 500 victory, Yarborough and Allison began fighting near the accident scene. After stopping to check on his brother, Bobby Allison began fighting with Yarborough, too. The race and fight were broadcast live on CBS, the first time a major race had been televised. The broadcast was the talk of the sports world for several days. When asked whether he'd fine Yarborough and the Allisons for fighting, NASCAR president Bill France Jr. reportedly said he should pay them for bringing so much attention to the sport.

The July 4, 1984, Firecracker 400 was the first time an American president had attended a stock car race. President Ronald Reagan gave the "Gentlemen, start your engines" command as he flew from Washington to Daytona Beach on Air Force 1. Two hours later, he watched from Bill France Sr.'s suite as Richard Petty beat Yarborough in a photo-finish. It was the last of Petty's record 200 NASCAR victories and the last of his 10 career victories at the speedway. Photos of France Sr. and Petty talking with President Reagan are an important piece of stock car history. Petty has always said that afternoon was the highlight of his outstanding stock car racing career.

Legendary driver Dale Earnhardt Sr. lost 19 consecutive Daytona 500s before finally winning in 1998. He was close several times, notably when a flat tire in the last turn on the last lap kept him from winning in 1990. He was second in 1984, 1993, 1995, and 1996 before breaking through. In 2001, running third on the last lap, he died when his car crashed in Turn 4 after contact with Sterling Marlin and Ken Schrader. The tragedy shocked the world and brought a rule requiring drivers in NASCAR's three major series to wear special head and neck protection. His death spurred research and development of energy-absorbing safety walls.

Today, the massive speedway stands in tribute to the France family and its vision for stock car racing. It's the main attraction on a complex that includes NASCAR's sprawling world headquarters and Daytona USA, a racing-related tourist attraction that includes displays, exhibits, gift shops, a theater, and museum. Many of the streets around the speedway

NASCAR driver Tom Pistone carried some extra safety equipment to the Daytona International Speedway in the late 1950s and early 1960s. He packed scuba gear and a life preserver in case his car crashed into Lake Lloyd, the 44-acre, 7-foot deep lake in the infield. Pistone, you see, couldn't swim, and he wasn't taking any chances.

Bill France Sr. built the 2.5-mile speedway in 1958 and opened it in February 1959. He and designer Charles Moneypenny used dirt and sand from a huge "borrow pit" near the backstretch to build the speedway's 31-degree banked turns. The lake was named for local automotive dealer J. Saxton Lloyd, a successful businessman who gave Bill France Sr. his first job in Daytona Beach in 1934. In the mid-1950s, Lloyd founded the Daytona Beach Racing and Recreation District and helped convince city officials that a large speedway for tens of thousands of fans would be great for the city's economy.

Lake Lloyd was 44 acres until late in 2004, when 15 acres were filled in. The dirt and sand came from the new vehicle and pedestrian tunnel built under Turn 1 in time for Speed Week 2005. The lake remains 3,000 feet long but isn't quite as wide as before. The 15 additional acres of shoreline provide enough space for 207 more recreation vehicles—at $990 each—to park along the lake. A Community Center, docks, and a beach-like recreation area have been added along the shoreline. The speedway now features water-skiing and wakeboarding shows during races. The lake is stocked with freshwater fish, but fans aren't allowed to fish off the docks.

Records are sketchy, but only two cars may have ended up in Lake Lloyd. (The speedway built a high, thick, dirt wall between the backstretch and the lake in the early 1990s.) In the mid-1960s, Bay Darnell spun off the backstretch and slid his ARCA car into the lake. About 30 years later, when the dirt wall wasn't high, Goody's Dash driver Dave Stacy spun and ended sliding slowly into the lake. Both drivers got wet but were otherwise uninjured.

Dale Earnhardt Sr. is ecstatic after winning the Daytona 500 in 1998. He had lost the previous 19 consecutive Daytona 500s. Three years later, he lost his life in the race when his car crashed in Turn 4.

are named in honor of the France family. That's only fitting since Bill France Sr. played such an important role in making Daytona Beach one of the world's most famous seaside cities.

Dozens of drivers had opinions about DIS when it opened in 1959. None of the opinions, however, seemed as appropriate as that of journeyman driver Jimmy Thompson. "There have been other tracks that separated the men from the boys," Thompson said before going out for his first time on the track. "This is the track that will separate the brave from the weak after the boys are gone."[4]

5

LOWE'S: EVERYBODY'S HOMETOWN TRACK

Though stock car racing was born in Daytona Beach, Florida, almost everyone considers Charlotte, North Carolina, its real hometown. After all, NASCAR's first major race was in June of 1949 on the three-quarter mile Charlotte Speedway. The half-mile Charlotte Fairgrounds on the other side of town had 17 races between 1954 and 1960, and Concord Speedway north of Charlotte had 11 races between 1956 and 1964. No other area in America has had nearly as many major stock car races since the sport's "formal" intro-duction in 1949. Today, most of NASCAR's best Nextel Cup, Busch, and Craftsman series teams are based in the Charlotte area. Almost 18,000 people in the area have racing-related jobs, and the sport pours almost $300 million into the area's economy each year.

At the heart of this growing industry is the Lowe's Motor Speedway (LMS). It's among stock car racing's most famous, successful and innovative facilities. Located in Concord, North Carolina, just north of Charlotte, the 1.5-mile, high-banked track was known as Charlotte Motor Speedway from

Jimmie Johnson, driver of the No. 48 Lowe's Chevrolet, takes the green flag for the start of the 2004 Coca-Cola 600 at Lowe's Motor Speedway in Concord, North Carolina. Johnson went on to win the race.

1960 through 1998. It became racing's first major facility with a corporate name when the Lowe's Home Improvement chain bought its naming rights in 1999.

The speedway hosts two Nextel Cup races each year. The first is a 400-lap, 600-miler on the last Sunday night of Memorial Day weekend in May. The race was called the World 600 from its debut in 1960 until 1985, when it became the Coca-Cola 600. Lowe's fall race began as a 400-miler in October of 1960 and stayed that distance until becoming a 500-miler in 1967. It was sponsored by a number of companies and products before the UAW-GM labor partnership bought the naming rights in 1995. LMS has hosted the Nextel All-Star Challenge (originally called The Winston) for 19 of the last 20 years, often with memorable results. The speedway also hosts races for the Busch and Craftsman series. In the past, it has presented major races for sports cars, open-wheel Indy Cars, several lower-level stock car series and the invitation-only International Race of Champions.

That's a pretty healthy lineup of events for a speedway that almost didn't survive its birth. Shortly after ground-breaking in July 1959, workers found almost a half-million cubic yards of solid granite. Track president Curtis Turner (a famous driver) and vice-president Bruton Smith (a successful short-track promoter) couldn't afford to fix the unexpected problem. Their entire construction budget was only $1 million, a huge sum at the time. The cost of blasting and removing the granite would be another $500,000. They raised the extra money by selling stock in their speedway corporation. Their first race, scheduled for May of 1960, was push to mid-June. It was scheduled for 600 miles, 100 miles longer than any oval-track race anywhere. Instead of calling it the Charlotte 600 or North Carolina 600, Turner and Smith called it the World 600.

"Promoting short-track events in the Charlotte area (before LMS), I learned you had to find something to make your race stand out," Smith said years later. "That's what we did with the 600. Darlington and Daytona Beach had both opened with 500-mile races. Indianapolis had been running 500-mile races for years. That distance had sort of become the standard. We knew that making our first race longer than the standard would separate us from the crowd. We actually thought briefly about just running 501 miles. Even though people thought we were crazy, we went with 600 miles. It's worked out really well."[5]

Despite still owing $500,000 in construction costs, Smith and Turner had enough money to post the purse, promote the race, and stage it. Joe Lee Johnson won by four laps, his first and only major NASCAR victory. He beat Johnny Beauchamp, Bobby Johns, Gerald Duke, and Buck Baker. The race attracted around 40,000 fans, considered good at the time. But Turner and Smith weren't able to pay all their labor and construction costs from ticket sales. They finally paid everyone, using $850,000 Turner borrowed from the Teamsters Union. The relationship between the speedway's ownership and Teamsters president Jimmy Hoffa bothered NASCAR president Bill France Sr. He was concerned that Hoffa would unionize the drivers and bring legalized gambling to the sport. He was so angry that he banned Turner from all NASCAR events from 1961 until late in 1965.

The loan helped the speedway survive its first year but only barely. In mid-1961, its board of directors grew restless because it seemed more money was going out than was coming in. Turner resigned from the board, but Smith stayed as general manager. The board of directors reluctantly put the speedway under Chapter 11 bankruptcy protection. (That's a legal procedure that helps businesses pay their creditors and reorganize their finances.) Robert N. Robinson, a Charlotte lawyer, was chosen to oversee the reorganization. In 1962, Charlotte businessman Richard Howard replaced Smith as the speedway's general manager. It took several years for Howard to get the speedway on a more solid financial basis.

After being replaced, Smith left North Carolina and began working in the retail automotive business. Despite having no plans to return to racing, he kept his speedway stock. In the early 1970s, several stockholders contacted Smith in Illinois and asked him to buy their stock. For the next few years, he bought out investors who weren't happy with the speedway's direction. He returned to Charlotte in 1974 and was elected chairman of the board of directors. By 1975, he'd bought enough stock to regain overall control of the speedway. He hired former sportswriter, public relations expert and short-track promoter H.A. "Humpy" Wheeler as his promotions manager. When Howard resigned after the 1975 season, Wheeler became the speedway's general manager.

Together, the men have changed how speedways do their business. Smith has spent tens of millions to improve LMS. In 1984, it became America's first sports facility with year-round living accommodations. Smith built 40 condominiums overlooking Turn 1 and made them available for public sale. In 1985, he built a private, country club-style restaurant called The Speedway Club overlooking the frontstretch. In 1988, he added Smith Tower, a 135,000-square-foot, seven-story facility connected to The Speedway Club and the main grandstand. The Tower houses the speedway's corporate offices, ticket office, souvenir gift shop, and leased office space.

In 1992, Smith spent $1.7 million for permanent lights, making LMS the first modern superspeedway with night racing. Today, both of its Nextel Cup races and the Nextel All-Star Challenge are run at night, in prime television time. In 2004, Smith spent $7.5 million for new rest rooms and showers for infield patrons. He built two 48-bay garages for competitors and a state-of-the-art media center. The speedway currently has 167,000 permanent seats stretching from Turn 4 all the way around to the middle of the backstretch.

Wheeler has become racing's most innovative and creative promoter. In the early 1980s, he began creating extravagant and flashy pre-race shows. LMS was the first track to make shows a major part of the race-day festivities. He's

Workers water down the asphalt in a process called "hydro cooling." With temperatures soaring to over 135 degrees, hydro cooling minimizes the rippling effect of heat waves coming off of the road surface.

brought in three-ring circuses, blockbuster musical acts, and long-distance jumps with school buses, junk cars and motorcycles. He's brought in enough Army and Marine helicopters, tanks, and armed personnel to fight a small war. He's had low-level jet flyovers and hundreds of skydivers. He's even hosted professional boxing matches for fans waiting for the race to begin.

His first big show was in the early 1980s, when the speedway was "invaded" by the 82nd Airborne from nearby Fort Bragg, North Carolina. Wheeler had a swarm of Apache and Chinook helicopters suddenly fly in from behind the Turn 4 grandstand. They dropped off soldiers and 105 howitzers,

Firemen raise a 50 x 30 foot American flag during pre-race ceremonies at Lowe's Motor Speedway. Thousands of uniformed firefighters participated in pre-race ceremonies to honor firefighters who were killed in the September 11 attacks.

and the howitzers began "firing" at a make-believe target outside the speedway. The crowd was taken by surprise because Wheeler and his staff had kept it a secret. Since then, fans have arrived early so they won't miss Wheeler's next spectacular.

"I think our best show was a month after 9/11 when we had 5,000 uniformed firefighters," Wheeler said. They were led by the guys from the Chinatown station in New York, the guys who were among the first at Ground Zero. Lee Greenwood sang three patriotic songs and we raised a huge American flag. The crowd went wild. One time I wanted to have a motorcyclist jump over a large pool of water with

Did you know?

Few people realized it at the time, but a light switch changed the face of stock car racing in May of 1992. That's when track owner Bruton Smith turned on 1,200 lights that illuminated Lowe's Motor Speedway (LMS) near Charlotte, North Carolina. The 1.5-mile facility was America's first superspeedway capable of hosting night races.

Its first major night-time event was the Winston All-Star race on Saturday night, May 16, 1992. Davey Allison won by inches after rallying from third in the final mile of the 105-mile race. Seconds later, after completing the race, he crashed into the outside wall after contact from Kyle Petty. Earlier on that last lap, leader Dale Earnhardt Sr. had spun while blocking Petty in Turn 3. When Petty slowed briefly, Allison passed in Turn 4 and went on to win. He suffered a broken collarbone and concussion in the post-race accident and spent that night and the next day in a hospital.

But the race was overshadowed by the lights. For years, short tracks across America had hosted night races. It was easy to light tracks shorter than a one-half

(Continued)

live sharks in it. I thought about it and thought about it, then decided it might not be such a good idea after all.

"Pre-race shows are important because racing is different from many other events. It's an experience, so it should be a grand one. When I went to races as a kid, I couldn't stand the wait before the start. The cars were too far away and it was boring. I think like a 12-year-old boy when it comes to what to give mile, but harder to light a 1.5-mile speedway with high-banked turns and 100,000 seats. Bruton Smith and track general manager Humpy Wheeler accepted the challenge to help their track keep the annual all-star race that several other tracks wanted.

The job cost almost $1.8 million and took several months. Musco Lighting of Iowa started by putting high-rise towers atop and behind the grandstands. That meant fans and television cameras didn't have to watch the race while dozens of poles interfered with their sightlines. Workers used shorter poles and ground-level mirrors to light the pit road, the turns, and the backstretch. Drivers said they could see as well at night as when they'd run afternoon races at LMS.

It wasn't long before other tracks installed lights. Today, short tracks at Bristol, Tennessee; Richmond, Virginia; and Martinsville, Virginia have them. The superspeedways at Hampton, Georgia; Fontana, California; Las Vegas, Nevada; Phoenix, Arizona; Loudon, New Hampshire; Fort Worth, Texas; Darlington, South Carolina; and Daytona Beach, Florida, have them. Lights have changed racing since they allow NASCAR to schedule major events at night when television ratings and advertisement revenue are higher.

fans on race day. They like stunts, military shows, and circus acts. People tell me about pre-race shows from 20 years ago but can't remember who won the race. Pre-race shows bring out the kid in people. Nobody has more fun than kids, especially 12-year-olds or adults who thinks like 12-year-olds."[6]

NOTES

Chapter 2

1. Al Pearce's personal interview with Darrell Waltrip, April 18, 1998 at Martinsville Speedway in Virginia.

Chapter 3

2. Al Pearce's personal interview with Ricky Rudd, March 21, 1997 at Darlington Raceway in South Carolina.

3. Al Pearce's personal interview with Junie Donlavey, March 3, 2005.

Chapter 4

4. Greg Fielden quoting Jimmy Thompson in *Forty Years of Stock Car Racing. The Superspeedway Boom 1959–1964* (Surfside Beach, SC: The Galfield Press, 1993), 11.

Chapter 5

5. Al Pearce's personal interview with Bruton Smith, January 25, 2005 at Lowe's Motor Speedway in Concord, North Carolina.

6. Al Pearce's personal interview with H.A. "Humpy" Wheeler, March 12, 2005 at Las Vegas Motor Speedway in Nevada.

CHRONOLOGY

1903 Ransom Olds and Alexander Winton begin pursuing land-speed records along the beach near Daytona Beach, Florida.

1936 Sir Malcolm Campbell makes his last land-speed record run on the beach near Daytona Beach, Florida.

The City of Daytona Beach stages the first race for street-legal, family passenger cars along a course that includes part of a public street and part of the nearby beach.

1947 H. Clay Earles builds Martinsville Speedway in Virginia.

1948 Bill France Sr. incorporates the National Association for Stock Car Auto Racing (NASCAR) in Daytona Beach, Florida.

1949 The "Strictly Stock" series (changed to Nextel Cup) debuts on a three-quarter mile dirt track in Charlotte, North Carolina. (The Nextel Cup was formerly known as the Winston Cup.)

1950 NASCAR's first paved superspeedway and its first 500-mile stock car race is run at Darlington Raceway in South Carolina.

1959 Bill France Sr. opens Daytona International Speedway with the first Daytona 500.

1960 Superspeedways open near Charlotte, North Carolina, and Atlanta, Georgia.

1965 NASCAR's newest superspeedway opens near Rockingham, North Carolina.

1969 Superspeedways open at four more sites: Dover, Delaware; Brooklyn, Michigan; Talladega, Alabama; and Bryan, Texas. The Texas track closes after the 1973 season.

1971 A major superspeedway opens at Ontario, California. It closes after the 1980 season.

1972 NASCAR founder Bill France Sr. gives control of the organization to his son, Bill France Jr.

1974 NASCAR runs its first race at Pocono Raceway in northeastern Pennsylvania.

1979 CBS-television has the first live, start-to-finish telecast of a major race, the Daytona 500.

1986 NASCAR returns to Watkins Glen, New York, the famous road circuit it had visited three times between 1957 and 1965.

1988 Paul Sawyer and his sons take seven months to refurbish the aging one-half mile State Fairgrounds Raceway into the three-quarter mile, state-of-the-art Richmond International Raceway in Virginia.

NASCAR makes inroads in the Southwest with its first race at Phoenix International Raceway in Arizona.

1989 Every major NASCAR race is televised, including NASCAR's first visit to Infineon Raceway at Sears Point, California.

1992 Lowe's Motor Speedway becomes the first super-speedway with lights, and promptly hosts the Nextel Challenge on a Saturday night.

1993 NASCAR takes its Nextel Cup series to New Hampshire International Speedway at Loudon.

1994 NASCAR runs its first race at the world-famous Indianapolis Motor Speedway in Indiana.

1997 Superspeedways open at Fort Worth, Texas, and Fontana, California.

1998 The Las Vegas Motor Speedway hosts its first Nextel Cup race.

1999 NASCAR runs its first Nextel Cup race at the Homestead-Miami Speedway in Florida.

With his health an issue, Bill France Jr., hands NASCAR's day-to-day responsibilities to senior vice-president Mike Helton.

2000 Mike Helton becomes president of NASCAR, the first non-France family member to hold the position.

2001 NASCAR takes its Nextel Cup series to the Chicagoland Speedway in Illinois and to Kansas Speedway near Kansas City.

2003 Brian Z. France becomes Chairman of the Board and CEO of NASCAR, replacing his father, Bill France Jr., as head of the organization.

2004 Nextel becomes the title sponsor of NASCAR's top series, replacing the Winston cigarette brand.

STATISTICS

Darlington Raceway

Harry Byrd Highway
Darlington, S.C. 29540
(886) 459-7223
www.darlingtonraceway.com
Owner: International Speedway Corp.
President: Chris Browning
Length: 1.366 miles
Turns 1-2 banking: 23 degrees
Turns 3-4 banking: 25 degrees
Straightaway banking: 2 degrees
Straightaway lengths: 1,229 feet
First race: September 1950
Permanent seats: 60,000

Nextel Cup Winners at Darlington Raceway:

Year	Race	Winner	Car
1950	Southern 500	Johnny Mantz	Plymouth
1951	Southern 500	Herb Thomas	Hudson
1952	Grand National 100	Dick Rathmann	Hudson
1952	Southern 500	Fonty Flock	Oldsmobile
1953	Southern 500	Buck Baker	Oldsmobile
1954	Southern 500	Herb Thomas	Hudson
1955	Southern 500	Herb Thomas	Chevrolet
1956	Southern 500	Curtis Turner	Ford
1957	Rebel 300	Fireball Roberts	Ford
1957	Southern 500	Speedy Thompson	Chevrolet
1958	Rebel 300	Curtis Turner	Ford
1958	Southern 500	Fireball Roberts	Chevrolet

1959	Rebel 300	Fireball Roberts	Chevrolet
1959	Southern 500	Jim Reed	Chevrolet
1960	Rebel 300	Joe Weatherly	Ford
1960	Southern 500	Buck Baker	Pontiac
1961	Rebel 300	Fred Lorenzen	Ford
1961	Southern 500	Nelson Stacy	Ford
1962	Rebel 300	Nelson Stacy	Ford
1962	Southern 500	Larry Frank	Ford
1963	Rebel 300	Joe Weatherly	Pontiac
1963	Southern 500	Fireball Roberts	Ford
1964	Rebel 300	Fred Lorenzen	Ford
1964	Southern 500	Buck Baker	Dodge
1965	Rebel 300	Junior Johnson	Ford
1965	Southern 500	Ned Jarrett	Ford
1966	Rebel 400	Richard Petty	Plymouth
1966	Southern 500	Darel Dieringer	Mercury
1967	Rebel 400	Richard Petty	Plymouth
1967	Southern 500	Richard Petty	Plymouth
1968	Rebel 400	David Pearson	Ford
1968	Southern 500	Cale Yarborough	Mercury
1969	Rebel 400	LeeRoy Yarbrough	Mercury
1969	Southern 500	LeeRoy Yarbrough	Ford
1970	Rebel 400	David Pearson	Ford
1970	Southern 500	Buddy Baker	Dodge
1971	Rebel 400	Buddy Baker	Dodge
1971	Southern 500	Bobby Allison	Mercury
1972	Rebel 500	David Pearson	Mercury
1972	Southern 500	Bobby Allison	Chevrolet
1973	Rebel 500	David Pearson	Mercury
1973	Southern 500	Cale Yarborough	Chevrolet
1974	Rebel 500	David Pearson	Mercury
1974	Southern 500	Cale Yarborough	Chevrolet

1977	Rebel 500	Darrell Waltrip	Chevrolet
1977	Southern 500	David Pearson	Mercury
1978	Rebel 500	Benny Parsons	Chevrolet
1978	Southern 500	Cale Yarborough	Oldsmobile
1979	CRC Rebel 500	Darrell Waltrip	Chevrolet
1979	Southern 500	David Pearson	Chevrolet
1980	CRC Rebel 500	David Pearson	Chevrolet
1980	Southern 500	Terry Labonte	Chevrolet
1981	CRC Rebel 500	Darrell Waltrip	Buick
1981	Southern 500	Neil Bonnett	Ford
1982	CRC Rebel 500	Dale Earnhardt Sr.	Ford
1982	Southern 500	Cale Yarborough	Buick
1983	TranSouth 500	Harry Gant	Buick
1983	Southern 500	Bobby Allison	Buick
1984	TranSouth 500	Darrell Waltrip	Chevrolet
1984	Southern 500	Harry Gant	Chevrolet
1985	TranSouth 500	Bill Elliott	Ford
1985	Southern 500	Bill Elliott	Ford
1986	TranSouth 500	Dale Earnhardt Sr.	Chevrolet
1986	Southern 500	Tim Richmond	Chevrolet
1987	TranSouth 500	Dale Earnhardt Sr.	Chevrolet
1987	Southern 500	Dale Earnhardt Sr.	Chevrolet
1988	TranSouth 500	Lake Speed	Oldsmobile
1988	Southern 500	Bill Elliott	Ford
1989	TranSouth 500	Harry Gant	Oldsmobile
1989	Heinz 500	Dale Earnhardt Sr.	Chevrolet
1990	TranSouth 500	Dale Earnhardt Sr.	Chevrolet
1990	Heinz 500	Dale Earnhardt Sr.	Chevrolet
1991	TranSouth 500	Ricky Rudd	Chevrolet
1991	Heinz 500	Harry Gant	Oldsmobile
1992	TranSouth 500	Bill Elliott	Ford
1992	Mt. Dew 500	Darrell Waltrip	Chevrolet

1993	TranSouth 500	Dale Earnhardt Sr.	Chevrolet
1993	Mt. Dew 500	Mark Martin	Ford
1994	TranSouth 500	Dale Earnhardt Sr.	Chevrolet
1994	Mt. Dew 500	Bill Elliott	Ford
1995	TranSouth 500	Sterling Marlin	Chevrolet
1995	Mt. Dew 500	Jeff Gordon	Chevrolet
1996	TranSouth 500	Jeff Gordon	Chevrolet
1996	Mt. Dew 500	Jeff Gordon	Chevrolet
1997	TranSouth 400	Dale Jarrett	Ford
1997	Southern 500	Jeff Gordon	Chevrolet
1998	TranSouth 500	Dale Jarrett	Ford
1998	Pepsi Southern 500	Jeff Gordon	Chevrolet
1999	TranSouth 500	Jeff Burton	Ford
1999	Pepsi Southern 500	Jeff Burton	Ford
2000	Mall.com 400	Ward Burton	Pontiac
2000	Pepsi Southern 500	Bobby Labonte	Pontiac
2001	Dodge Dealers 400	Dale Jarrett	Ford
2001	Mt. Dew Southern 500	Ward Burton	Pontiac
2002	Dodge Dealers 400	Sterling Marlin	Dodge
2002	Mt. Dew Southern 500	Jeff Gordon	Chevrolet
2003	Dodge Dealers 400	Ricky Craven	Pontiac
2003	Mt. Dew Southern 500	Terry Labonte	Chevrolet
2004	Dodge Dealers 400	Jimmie Johnson	Chevrolet
2004	Mt. Dew Southern 500	Jimmie Johnson	Chevrolet

Top-5 winners: David Pearson (10), Dale Earnhardt Sr. (9), Jeff Gordon (6), and Cale Yarborough, Bobby Allison, Darrell Waltrip, and Bill Elliott (5 each)

Top-5 pole winners: David Pearson (12), Fireball Roberts (7), Fred Lorenzen (6), Bill Elliott (5) and Richard Petty, Bobby Allison, and Geoffrey Bodine (4 each)

Track qualifying record: 173.797 mph by Ward Burton in March of 1996

Track race record: 139.958 mph by Dale Earnhardt Sr. in March of 1993

Daytona International Speedway

1801 West International Speedway Blvd.
Daytona Beach, Fla. 32120
(386) 254-2700
www.daytonainternationalspeedway.com
Owner: International Speedway Corp.
President: Robin Braig
Length: 2.5 miles
Corner banking: 31 degrees
Backstretch banking: 3 degrees
Tri-oval banking: 18 degrees
Frontstretch length: 3,800 feet
Backstretch length: 3,400 feet
First race: February of 1959
Permanent seats: 168,000

Nextel Cup winners at Daytona International Speedway:

Year	Race	Winner	Car
1959	Daytona 500	Lee Petty	Oldsmobile
1959	Firecracker 250	Fireball Roberts	Pontiac
1960	Daytona 500	Junior Johnson	Chevrolet
1960	Firecracker 250	Jack Smith	Pontiac
1961	Daytona 500	Marvin Panch	Pontiac
1961	Firecracker 250	David Pearson	Pontiac
1962	Daytona 500	Fireball Roberts	Pontiac
1962	Firecracker 250	Fireball Roberts	Pontiac
1963	Daytona 500	Tiny Lund	Ford
1963	Firecracker 400	Fireball Roberts	Ford
1964	Daytona 500	Richard Petty	Plymouth
1964	Firecracker 400	A.J. Foyt	Dodge

1965	Daytona 500	Fred Lorenzen	Ford
1965	Firecracker 400	A.J. Foyt	Plymouth
1966	Daytona 500	Richard Petty	Plymouth
1966	Firecracker 400	Sam McQuagg	Dodge
1967	Daytona 500	Mario Andretti	Ford
1967	Firecracker 400	Cale Yarborough	Ford
1968	Daytona 500	Cale Yarborough	Mercury
1968	Firecracker 400	Cale Yarborough	Mercury
1969	Daytona 500	LeeRoy Yarbrough	Ford
1969	Firecracker 400	LeeRoy Yarbrough	Ford
1970	Daytona 500	Pete Hamilton	Plymouth
1970	Firecracker 400	Donnie Allison	Ford
1971	Daytona 500	Richard Petty	Plymouth
1971	Firecracker 400	Bobby Isaac	Dodge
1972	Daytona 500	A.J. Foyt	Mercury
1972	Firecracker 400	David Pearson	Mercury
1973	Daytona 500	Richard Petty	Dodge
1973	Firecracker 400	David Pearson	Mercury
1974	Daytona 500	Richard Petty	Dodge
1974	Firecracker 400	David Pearson	Mercury
1975	Daytona 500	Benny Parsons	Chevrolet
1975	Firecracker 400	Richard Petty	Dodge
1976	Daytona 500	David Pearson	Mercury
1976	Firecracker 400	Cale Yarborough	Chevrolet
1977	Daytona 500	Cale Yarborough	Chevrolet
1977	Firecracker 400	Richard Petty	Dodge
1978	Daytona 500	Bobby Allison	Ford
1978	Firecracker 400	David Pearson	Mercury
1979	Daytona 500	Richard Petty	Oldsmobile
1979	Firecracker 400	Neil Bonnett	Mercury
1980	Daytona 500	Buddy Baker	Oldsmobile
1980	Firecracker 400	Bobby Allison	Mercury

1981	Daytona 500	Richard Petty	Buick
1981	Firecracker 400	Cale Yarborough	Buick
1982	Daytona 500	Bobby Allison	Buick
1982	Firecracker 400	Bobby Allison	Buick
1983	Daytona 500	Cale Yarborough	Pontiac
1983	Firecracker 400	Buddy Baker	Ford
1984	Daytona 500	Cale Yarborough	Chevrolet
1984	Pepsi 400	Richard Petty	Pontiac
1985	Daytona 500	Bill Elliott	Ford
1985	Pepsi 400	Greg Sacks	Chevrolet
1986	Daytona 500	Geoffrey Bodine	Chevrolet
1986	Pepsi 400	Tim Richmond	Chevrolet
1987	Daytona 500	Bill Elliott	Ford
1987	Pepsi 400	Bobby Allison	Buick
1988	Daytona 500	Bobby Allison	Buick
1988	Pepsi 400	Bill Elliott	Ford
1989	Daytona 500	Darrell Waltrip	Chevrolet
1989	Pepsi 400	Davey Allison	Ford
1990	Daytona 500	Derrike Cope	Chevrolet
1990	Pepsi 400	Dale Earnhardt Sr.	Chevrolet
1991	Daytona 500	Ernie Irvan	Chevrolet
1991	Pepsi 400	Bill Elliott	Ford
1992	Daytona 500	Davey Allison	Ford
1992	Pepsi 400	Ernie Irvan	Chevrolet
1993	Daytona 500	Dale Jarrett	Chevrolet
1993	Pepsi 400	Dale Earnhardt Sr.	Chevrolet
1994	Daytona 500	Sterling Marlin	Chevrolet
1994	Pepsi 400	Jimmy Spencer	Ford
1995	Daytona 500	Sterling Marlin	Chevrolet
1995	Pepsi 400	Jeff Gordon	Chevrolet
1996	Daytona 500	Dale Jarrett	Ford
1996	Pepsi 400	Sterling Marlin	Chevrolet

1997	Daytona 500	Jeff Gordon	Chevrolet
1997	Pepsi 400	John Andretti	Ford
1998	Daytona 500	Dale Earnhardt Sr.	Chevrolet
1998	Pepsi 400	Jeff Gordon	Chevrolet
2000	Daytona 500	Dale Jarrett	Ford
2000	Pepsi 400	Jeff Burton	Ford
2001	Daytona 500	Michael Waltrip	Chevrolet
2001	Pepsi 400	Dale Earnhardt Jr.	Chevrolet
2002	Daytona 500	Ward Burton	Pontiac
2002	Pepsi 400	Michael Waltrip	Chevrolet
2003	Daytona 500	Michael Waltrip	Chevrolet
2003	Pepsi 400	Greg Biffle	Ford
2004	Daytona 500	Dale Earnhardt Jr.	Chevrolet
2004	Pepsi 400	Jeff Gordon	Chevrolet

Top-5 winners: Richard Petty (10), Cale Yarborough (8), David Pearson and Bobby Allison (6 each), Jeff Gordon (4)

Top-5 pole winners: Cale Yarborough (12), Buddy Baker, Fireball Roberts, and Bill Elliott (5 each), Donnie Allison (4), Ken Schrader and Sterling Marlin (4 each)

Track qualifying record: 210.364 mph by Bill Elliott in February of 1987

Track race record: 177.602 mph by Buddy Baker in February of 1980

Lowe's Motor Speedway

U.S. 29 and Morehead Road
Concord, N.C. 28027
(704) 455-3200
www.lowesmotorspeedway.com
Owner: Speedway Motorsports Inc.
President: H.A. "Humpy" Wheeler
Length: 1.5 miles
Corner banking: 24 degrees

Frontstretch banking: 5 degrees
Backstretch banking: 5 degrees
Frontstretch length: 1,952 feet
Backstretch length: 1,360 feet
First race: June 1960
Permanent seats: 171,000

Nextel Cup winners at Lowe's Motor Speedway:

Year	Race	Winner	Car
1960	World 600	Joe Lee Johnson	Chevrolet
1960	National 400	Speedy Thompson	Ford
1961	World 600	David Pearson	Pontiac
1961	National 400	Joe Weatherly	Pontiac
1962	World 600	Nelson Stacy	Ford
1962	National 400	Junior Johnson	Pontiac
1963	World 600	Fred Lorenzen	Ford
1963	National 40	Junior Johnson	Chevrolet
1964	World 600	Jim Paschal	Plymouth
1964	National 400	Fred Lorenzen	Ford
1965	World 600	Fred Lorenzen	Ford
1965	National 500	Fred Lorenzen	Ford
1966	World 600	Marvin Panch	Plymouth
1966	National 500	LeeRoy Yarbrough	Dodge
1967	World 600	Jim Paschal	Plymouth
1967	National 500	Buddy Baker	Dodge
1968	World 600	Buddy Baker	Dodge
1968	National 500	Charlie Glotzbach	Dodge
1969	World 600	LeeRoy Yarbrough	Mercury
1969	National 500	Donnie Allison	Ford
1970	World 600	Donnie Allison	Ford
1970	National 500	LeeRoy Yarbrough	Mercury
1971	World 600	Bobby Allison	Mercury

1971	National 500	Bobby Allison	Mercury
1972	World 600	Buddy Baker	Dodge
1972	National 500	Bobby Allison	Chevrolet
1973	World 600	Buddy Baker	Dodge
1973	National 500	Cale Yarborough	Chevrolet
1974	World 600	David Pearson	Mercury
1974	National 500	David Pearson	Mercury
1975	World 600	Richard Petty	Dodge
1975	National 500	Richard Petty	Dodge
1976	World 600	David Pearson	Mercury
1976	National 500	Donnie Allison	Chevrolet
1977	World 600	Richard Petty	Dodge
1977	All-Pro 500	Benny Parsons	Chevrolet
1978	World 600	Darrell Waltrip	Chevrolet
1978	All-Pro 500	Bobby Allison	Ford
1979	World 600	Darrell Waltrip	Chevrolet
1979	National 500	Cale Yarborough	Chevrolet
1980	World 600	Benny Parsons	Chevrolet
1980	National 500	Dale Earnhardt Sr.	Chevrolet
1981	World 600	Bobby Allison	Buick
1981	National 500	Darrell Waltrip	Buick
1982	World 600	Neil Bonnett	Ford
1982	National 500	Harry Gant	Buick
1983	World 600	Neil Bonnett	Chevrolet
1983	Miller 500	Richard Petty	Oldsmobile
1984	World 600	Bobby Allison	Buick
1984	Miller 500	Bill Elliott	Ford
1985	World 600	Darrell Waltrip	Chevrolet
1985	Miller 500	Cale Yarborough	Ford
1986	Coca-Cola 600	Dale Earnhardt Sr.	Chevrolet
1986	Oakwood 500	Dale Earnhardt Sr.	Chevrolet
1987	Coca-Cola 600	Kyle Petty	Ford

1987	Oakwood 500	Bill Elliott	Ford
1989	Coca-Cola 600	Darrell Waltrip	Chevrolet
1989	All-Pro 500	Ken Schrader	Chevrolet
1990	Coca-Cola 600	Rusty Wallace	Pontiac
1990	Mello Yello 500	Davey Allison	Ford
1991	Coca-Cola 600	Davey Allison	Ford
1991	Mello Yello 500	Geoffrey Bodine	Ford
1992	Coca-Cola 600	Dale Earnhardt Sr.	Chevrolet
1992	Mello Yello 500	Mark Martin	Ford
1993	Coca-Cola 600	Dale Earnhardt Sr.	Chevrolet
1993	Mello Yello 500	Ernie Irvan	Ford
1994	Coca-Cola 600	Jeff Gordon	Chevrolet
1994	Mello Yello 500	Dale Jarrett	Ford
1995	Coca-Cola 600	Bobby Labonte	Chevrolet
1995	UAW-GM 500	Mark Martin	Ford
1996	Coca-Cola 600	Dale Jarrett	Ford
1996	UAW-GM 500	Terry Labonte	Chevrolet
1997	Coca-Cola 600	Jeff Gordon	Chevrolet
1997	UAW-GM 500	Dale Jarrett	Ford
1998	Coca-Cola 600	Jeff Gordon	Chevrolet
1998	UAW-GM 500	Mark Martin	Ford
1999	Coca-Cola 600	Jeff Burton	Ford
1999	UAW-GM 500	Jeff Gordon	Chevrolet
2000	Coca-Cola 600	Matt Kenseth	Ford
2000	UAW-GM 500	Bobby Labonte	Pontiac
2001	Coca-Cola 600	Jeff Burton	Ford
2001	UAW-GM 500	Sterling Marlin	Dodge
2002	Coca-Cola 600	Mark Martin	Ford
2002	UAW-GM 500	Jamie McMurray	Dodge
2003	Coca-Cola 600	Jimmie Johnson	Chevrolet
2003	UAW-GM 500	Tony Stewart	Chevrolet
2004	Coca-Cola 600	Jimmie Johnson	Chevrolet

2004   UAW-GM 500   Jimmie Johnson   Chevrolet

Top-5 winners: Bobby Allison and Darrell Waltrip (6 each), Dale Earnhardt Sr. (5), and Jeff Gordon, David Pearson, Buddy Baker, Fred Lorenzen, Richard Petty, and Mark Martin (4 each)

Top-5 pole winners: David Pearson (14), Jeff Gordon (7), Bill Elliott, Cale Yarborough, and Charlie Glotzbach (4 each)

Track qualifying record: 188.877 mph by Ryan Newman in October of 2004

Track race record: 160.306 mph by Jeff Gordon in October of 1999

Martinsville Speedway

U.S. 220 South
Martinsville, Va. 24112
(877) 722-3859
www.martinsvillespeedway.com
Owner: International Speedway Corporation
President: Clay Campbell
Length: .526-mile
Corner banking: 12 degrees
Straightaway banking: 0 degrees
Straightaway lengths: 800 feet
First NASCAR race: September 1949
Permanent seats: 91,000

Nextel Cup winners at Martinsville Speedway:

Year	Race	Winner	Car
1949	Strictly Stock 200	Red Byron	Oldsmobile
1950	Grand National 150	Curtis Turner	Oldsmobile
1950	Grand National 150	Herb Thomas	Plymouth

1951	Grand National 200	Curtis Turner	Oldsmobile
1951	Grand National 200	Frank Mundy	Oldsmobile
1952	Grand National 200	Dick Rathmann	Hudson
1952	Grand National 200	Herb Thomas	Hudson
1953	Grand National 200	Lee Petty	Dodge
1953	Grand National 200	Jim Paschal	Dodge
1954	Grand National 200	Jim Paschal	Oldsmobile
1954	Grand National 200	Lee Petty	Chrysler
1955	Grand National 200	Tim Flock	Chrysler
1955	Grand National 200	Speedy Thompson	Chrysler
1956	Virginia 500	Buck Baker	Dodge
1956	Old Dominion 500	Jack Smith	Dodge
1957	Virginia 500	Buck Baker	Chevrolet
1957	Old Dominion 500	Bob Welborn	Chevrolet
1958	Virginia 500	Bob Welborn	Chevrolet
1958	Old Dominion 500	Fireball Roberts	Chevrolet
1959	Virginia 500	Lee Petty	Oldsmobile
1959	Old Dominion 500	Rex White	Chevrolet
1960	Virginia 500	Richard Petty	Plymouth
1960	Old Dominion 500	Rex White	Chevrolet
1961	Virginia 500	Fred Lorenzen	Ford
1961	Va. Sweepstakes 500	Junior Johnson	Pontiac
1961	Old Dominion 500	Joe Weatherly	Pontiac
1962	Virginia 500	Richard Petty	Plymouth
1962	Old Dominion 500	Nelson Stacy	Ford
1963	Virginia 500	Richard Petty	Plymouth
1963	Old Dominion 500	Fred Lorenzen	Ford
1964	Virginia 500	Fred Lorenzen	Ford
1964	Old Dominion 500	Fred Lorenzen	Ford
1965	Virginia 500	Fred Lorenzen	Ford
1965	Old Dominion 500	Junior Johnson	Ford
1966	Virginia 500	Jim Paschal	Plymouth
1966	Old Dominion 500	Fred Lorenzen	Ford

1967	Virginia 500	Richard Petty	Plymouth
1967	Old Dominion 500	Richard Petty	Plymouth
1968	Virginia 500	Cale Yarborough	Mercury
1968	Old Dominion 500	Richard Petty	Plymouth
1969	Virginia 500	Richard Petty	Ford
1969	Old Dominion 500	Richard Petty	Ford
1970	Virginia 500	Bobby Isaac	Dodge
1970	Old Dominion 500	Richard Petty	Plymouth
1971	Virginia 500	Richard Petty	Plymouth
1971	Old Dominion 500	Bobby Isaac	Dodge
1972	Virginia 500	Richard Petty	Plymouth
1972	Old Dominion 500	Richard Petty	Plymouth
1973	Virginia 500	David Pearson	Mercury
1973	Old Dominion 500	Richard Petty	Dodge
1974	Virginia 500	Cale Yarborough	Mercury
1974	Old Dominion 500	Earl Ross	Chevrolet
1975	Virginia 500	Richard Petty	Plymouth
1975	Old Dominion 500	Dave Marcis	Dodge
1976	Virginia 500	Darrell Waltrip	Chevrolet
1976	Old Dominion 500	Cale Yarborough	Chevrolet
1977	Virginia 500	Cale Yarborough	Chevrolet
1977	Old Dominion 500	Cale Yarborough	Chevrolet
1978	Virginia 500	Darrell Waltrip	Chevrolet
1978	Old Dominion 500	Cale Yarborough	Oldsmobile
1979	Virginia 500	Richard Petty	Chevrolet
1979	Old Dominion 500	Buddy Baker	Chevrolet
1980	Virginia 500	Darrell Waltrip	Chevrolet
1980	Old Dominion 500	Dale Earnhardt Sr.	Chevrolet
1981	Virginia 500	Morgan Shepherd	Pontiac
1981	Old Dominion 500	Darrell Waltrip	Buick
1982	Va. National Bank 500	Harry Gant	Buick
1982	Old Dominion 500	Darrell Waltrip	Buick

1983	Va. National Bank 500	Darrell Waltrip	Chevrolet
1983	Goody's 500	Ricky Rudd	Chevrolet
1984	Sovran Bank 500	Geoffrey Bodine	Chevrolet
1984	Goody's 500	Darrell Waltrip	Chevrolet
1985	Sovran Bank 500	Harry Gant	Chevrolet
1985	Goody's 500	Dale Earnhardt Sr.	Chevrolet
1986	Sovran Bank 500	Ricky Rudd	Ford
1986	Goody's 500	Rusty Wallace	Pontiac
1987	Sovran Bank 500	Dale Earnhardt Sr.	Chevrolet
1987	Goody's 500	Darrell Waltrip	Chevrolet
1988	Pannill 500	Dale Earnhardt Sr.	Chevrolet
1988	Goody's 500	Darrell Waltrip	Chevrolet
1989	Pannill 500	Darrell Waltrip	Chevrolet
1989	Goody's 500	Darrell Waltrip	Chevrolet
1990	Hanes 500	Geoffrey Bodine	Ford
1990	Goody's 500	Geoffrey Bodine	Ford
1991	Hanes 500	Dale Earnhardt Sr.	Chevrolet
1991	Goody's 500	Harry Gant	Oldsmobile
1992	Hanes 500	Mark Martin	Ford
1992	Goody's 500	Geoffrey Bodine	Ford
1993	Hanes 500	Rusty Wallace	Ford
1993	Goody's 500	Ernie Irvan	Ford
1994	Hanes	Rusty Wallace	Ford
1994	Goody's 500	Rusty Wallace	Ford
1995	Hanes 500	Rusty Wallace	Ford
1995	Goody's 500	Dale Earnhardt	Chevrolet
1996	Goody's 500	Rusty Wallace	Ford
1996	Hanes 500	Jeff Gordon	Chevrolet
1997	Goody's 500	Jeff Gordon	Chevrolet
1997	Hanes 500	Jeff Burton	Ford
1998	Goody's 500	Bobby Hamilton	Chevrolet
1998	NAPA 500	Ricky Rudd	Ford

1999	Goody's 500	John Andretti	Pontiac
1999	NAPA 500	Jeff Gordon	Chevrolet
2000	Goody's 500	Mark Martin	Ford
2000	NAPA 500	Tony Stewart	Pontiac
2001	Virginia 500	Dale Jarrett	Ford
2001	Old Dominion 500	Ricky Craven	Ford
2002	Virginia 500	Bobby Labonte	Pontiac
2002	Old Dominion	Kurt Busch	Ford
2003	Virginia 500	Jeff Gordon	Chevrolet
2003	Subway 500	Jeff Gordon	Chevrolet
2004	Advance Parts 500	Rusty Wallace	Dodge
2004	Subway 500	Jimmie Johnson	Chevrolet

Top-5 winners: Richard Petty (15), Darrell Waltrip (11), Rusty Wallace (7), Cale Yarborough and Dale Earnhardt Sr. (6 each)

Top-5 pole winners: Darrell Waltrip (8), Geoffrey Bodine (7), Cale Yarborough, Glen Wood, and Jeff Gordon (5 each)

Track qualifying record: 97.043 mph; Ryan Newman in October of 2004

Track race record: 82.223 mph by Jeff Gordon in September of 1996

GLOSSARY

Backstretch: The straight portion of a speedway farthest away from the start/finish line and the main grandstands. Sometimes called the "back straightaway," cars begin their run down the backstretch when they exit Turn 2. The entrance to Turn 3 marks the end of the backstretch.

Banking: The degree to which the racing surface of a speedway is angled away from the flat portion of the track in the turns. The largest turns on the 2.5-mile speedway at Daytona Beach, Florida, are angled at 31 degrees, almost too steep to walk up. In contrast, the turns at the half-mile Martinsville Speedway in Virginia are banked at 12 degrees.

Frontstretch: The straight portion of a speedway in front of the largest grandstand. The press box, VIP suites, and the race control booth generally overlook the frontstretch. The start/finish line is on the frontstretch, which is also sometimes called the "main straightaway." Cars approach the frontstretch by exiting Turn 4 and leave the frontstretch when they enter Turn 1.

Grand National: The name of NASCAR's top series from 1950 through the 1973 seasons.

NASCAR: The National Association for Stock Car Auto Racing was formed in December of 1947 and incorporated early in 1948. It was founded and remains based in Daytona Beach, Florida. Bill France Sr.

created NASCAR to organize, promote, and conduct stock car races. NASCAR has crowned a National Champion, made and enforced rules, monitored the safety of competitors and spectators, and ensured that speedways running NASCAR races paid the proper purse and conducted the races fairly.

Nextel Cup: The name currently used for NASCAR's top series. The 2004 season was the first under the sponsorship of telecommunications company Nextel.

Start/finish line: The place along the frontstretch where all races begin and end. The starter and his assistant are on a flagstand a few feet above the track at the start/finish line. They use a green flag to start the race and a checkered flag to end it. The race is scored by officials seated in the scoring stand in a special booth overlooking the start/finish line.

Strictly Stock: The name of NASCAR's top series during the 1949 season. The cars were street-legal, family sedans with little or no modifications to make them race cars.

Tri-oval: The portion of a speedway's frontstretch that's pulled slightly away from the pit road. Instead of an oval, the track begins to look something like a triangle. In most cases, the start/finish line is at the precise point on the frontstretch that is farthest from pit road.

Winston Cup: The name of NASCAR's top series between 1971 and 2003. The series was sponsored throughout that time by the Winston brand of the R.J. Reynolds Tobacco Company.

FURTHER READING

Fielden, Greg. *Forty Years of Stock Car Racing: The Beginning 1949–1958.* Surfside Beach, SC: The Galfield Press, 1987.

Forty Years of Stock Car Racing: The Superspeedway Boom 1959–1964. Surfside Beach, SC: The Galfield Press, 1993.

Fleischman, Bill and Al Pearce. *Inside NASCAR. The Ultimate Fan Guide.* Detroit, MI: The Gale Group, 2004.

Golenbach, Peter and Greg Fielden. *The Stock Car Racing Encyclopedia.* Indianapolis, IN: Macmillan, 1997.

Hunter, Don and Al Pearce. *The Illustrated History of Stock Car Racing. From The Sands of Daytona to Madison Avenue.* Osceola, WI: Motorbooks International Publishing, 1998.

Knechel, Samuel W. *NAPA Almanac of Stock Car Racing 1947–1997.* Atlanta, GA: National Automotive Parts Association, 1998.

NASCAR media relations staff. *2005 NASCAR Nextel Cup Media Guide.* Daytona Beach, FL: National Association for Stock Car Auto Racing, 2005.

Sowers, Richard. *The Complete Statistical History of Stock-Car Racing.* Phoenix, AZ: David Bull Publishing, 2000.

Stephenson, Morris and Dick Thompson. *From Dust To Glory. The Story of Clay Earles and the NASCAR-Sanctioned Martinsville Speedway*. Bassett, VA: The Bassett Printing Corp., 1992.

Winfrey, Sarona, Brian Briscoe, and Gary Guehler. *2005 Texas Motor Speedway Industry Contact Book*. Fort Worth, TX: Sprint Press, 2005.

BIBLIOGRAPHY

Fielden, Greg. *Forty Years of Stock Car Racing:*
The Superspeedway Boom 1959–1964. Surfside Beach,
South Carolina: The Galfield Press, 1993.

Photo Credits:

ADDRESSES

NASCAR
P.O. Box 2875
Daytona Beach, FL 32120
(386) 253-0611

Martinsville Speedway
U.S. 220 South
Martinsville, VA 24112
(877) 722-3859

Darlington Raceway
Harry Byrd Highway
Darlington, SC 29540
(886) 459-7223

Daytona International Speedway
P.O. Box 2801
Daytona Beach, FL 32120-2801
(386) 254-2700

Lowe's Motor Speedway
U.S. 29 and Morehead Road
Concord, NC 28027
(704) 455-3200

INTERNET SITES

www.nascar.com

> *This website the best place to start learning more about NASCAR. NASCAR stands for the National Association for Stock Car Auto Racing. NASCAR's site has the latest results and driver standings, and it also has pages where readers can learn more about the sport in general.*

www.martinsvillespeedway.com

> *This is the website for Martinsville Speedway, located in Martinsville, Virginia.*

www.darlingtonraceway.com

> *This is the website for Darlington Raceway, located in Darlington, South Carolina.*

www.daytonainternationalspeedway.com

> *This is the website for Daytona International Speedway, located in Daytona, Florida.*

www.lowesmotorspeedway.com

> *This is the official website for Lowe's Motor Speedway, located in Concord, North Carolina.*

INDEX

ABOUT THE AUTHOR

Al Pearce has authored or co-authored more than a dozen books about stock car racing. He covered the sport for more than 35 years for the *Daily Press* of Newport News, Virginia, and has covered NASCAR for *Auto Week* magazine since 1971. He received the Henry McLemore Award and was inducted into the Media Wing of the International Motorsports Hall of Fame at Talladega, Alabama, in the spring of 2004. He lives in Newport News, Virginia, with his wife, Francie, their teenage daughter, Annie, a dog, and an Arabian show horse.